Little Man in a Dog Suit:

The Story of a Boston Terrier

By B. R. Wilson

SpiritBooks
wilson@spiritbooks.me

1.Boston Terrier 2. Dogs 3. Oregon coast 4. Animals 5. Animal Intelligence 6. Dog socialization 7. Dog surgery

Cover design by Tamaris Johnson
Photo by Jeff Davis
First edition 2011

ISBN 978-0-9834956-5-9

For Frank and Reggie Wilson

Table of Contents

My Pack:

Tank, Tina, Bee, Frank, and Me

Chapter One
Puppyhood

My coming into the world was not the usual easy matter. Others in the litter popped out like rabbits from a burrow, but not me. Even then, I was different. Being the runt can turn a dog bitter, make him timid, or bring out a noble character. In my case, it was nobility. Size is useful to a Boston, for it may well determine who will win a fight. And as my flattened nose suggests, I was bred to be a warrior.

The first Boston terriers were fighting dogs, and they were twice as big as my parents. Long ago, somebody in Boston bred a big English bulldog/English terrier mix with a small white female named Gyp. She had a face like a bulldog, with an ugly underbite and a squarish head. The combination would not seem very promising in the looks department, but help was on the way. Out of Gyp's litter came my ancestors, who were bred with elegant French bulldogs belonging to local aristocrats. The result was a compact, wiry, round-headed, feisty little dog that could be depended on to fight and win. The result was me.

My ancestors were bred by common coachmen and barbers. Servants used to sneak tough pit dogs out of and into the great houses, determined to breed animals that would make them big money. Some dogs turned out to be fine ratters in coalmines and factories, a job that depended on courage and speed. Others became winners in the dog-fight pits and led grim, gladiatorial lives that were usually painful and short.

I carried the bloodlines and character of them all—the instinct to take out rodents, the urge to battle when challenged, the polite, obedient manner of the drawing room. You might say I was a study in contrasts, as is my breed. Above all, we are intelligent and wily, with minds of our own. Obedience is all very well, but in a fight, you have to make quick decisions or you're dead. I would rather take charge of circumstances than wind up as their victim.

Some circumstances are not a choice, however, but are thrust upon us. Birth is one of them. While I lay stuck inside my mother, rump backward, I had plenty of time to reflect on my situation. Maybe being stuck leads a fellow to become a thinker, since that's what I was from the start. Other dogs seem to act first and think later, but not me. Adaptability, I've always thought, is the highest form of intelligence, requiring one to consider alternatives and make choices. The problem with birth is that your choices are limited, as is your field of action.

Figuring that my hind quarters were the problem, I scrunched together, making myself as small as I could. This strategy didn't help, since the tunnel pressing around me just got smaller too. Finally, when I had run out of options and was starting to choke, something pressed hard around my hips and lower back, so hard I wanted to yelp. My mouth, however, was full of yuck, preventing any sound. I was being pulled backward by what I later learned was a human hand, not as gently as I would have liked. My whole lower body felt like it had been squished into half its proper size and it hurt, even after I had been pulled out. It went on hurting, but I got used to it. Of this significant event and its consequences, more later.

My stomach was small too, and I struggled with my litter mates to find some food. We rooted at our mother's milk supply and kicked each other away when we finally got a teat of our own. The worst offender was Julius, my biggest brother, who had a powerful kick that often landed in my face, squishing my nose flatter than was right, even for a Boston Terrier. Because I was the runt, I had the hardest time getting my fair share. Fighting for a teat gave me time to think before I ate, while the others guzzled mindlessly away. I had to plan which teat I would go for, which usually meant finding the one under our mother's leg. Being little was an advantage in going for this one, since no one else could fit in the tight space.

We must have been an absurd sight, the six of us squealing, kicking, and sucking. Our faces were covered with milk, so you could hardly see the black markings on our round little heads. All of us had a neat white streak down the center of our faces and a white bib. The rest of each body was black as a tuxedo, which our breeder said was just as it should be. That was a relief to hear, as I already felt a bit nervous about being so small. It was good to know nothing else was wrong with me. Well, there was the matter of hindquarters that hurt, but because of all the other excitement in my life, the pain went to the back of my mind and stayed there. I was much more interested in the boxful of puppies.

We huddled around each other to sleep, everyone pushing for the spot in the middle. Once again, my planning paid off. Because I was little, I could squiggle in between and underneath the others, thereby reaching the warmest, most secure spot, smack in the middle, next to my favorite mate, Dorothy. She always moved over a bit, letting me find a comfortable place. Because of my sore hindquarters, finding a comfortable place was always a big deal to me, even after I got my own human and home and bed, as will become clear.

At first, our lives were limited by the walls of the whelping box and the milk supply from our mother. I explored the borders of the box, having a faint sense even then that being on patrol was a duty expected of responsible dogs. The others sometimes did it too, but mostly relied on me to keep watch. Even then, I felt like I was destined to rule as an alpha, despite my size. I gave the matter considerable thought, since the whelping box didn't offer me much of a challenge.

A whole world opened up for me when we were allowed out of our box. Mother wandered off into the farm's meadow and expected us to follow. For the most part, I did, wanting to be sure that my food supply was close at hand. But while the others picked up their feet high to trot through the tall grass, I ran this way and that, sometimes standing on my hind legs to see over the blades. Since it hurt to stand up, I did it only for a minute, then rushed off to see what else there was out there. Sometimes I saw horses, which I at first mistook for very large dogs. When I saw humans climb up and ride them, I realized I was wrong. Would I ever get that big? I wasn't sure, but it seemed unlikely. My mother was nowhere near as big as a horse, and she was fully grown. So I gave up the dream of turning into a horse. Maybe something smaller. A pony perhaps, I thought, as I lay in the sunshine, warming my rear quarters so that they almost didn't hurt at all.

Then I spied a black and white dog, a giant among dogs, called Tiny by the man who walked with him on the farm. I didn't get the irony, since I was only a pup, not thinking as subtly as I would later. The giant dog was an old Dane, our man said, and was favored among all the other animals. I longed to be as big as Tiny, but knew even as a pup that this was a pipedream. I'd be lucky to get as big as Mother, who came up no farther than Tiny's dew claws. To make me feel better about my size, the farm family had started calling me Reggie, a name I gather had some royal connotations and suited my alpha character.

Best of all, I liked the little boy who came out to play with the litter as soon as we were allowed outside the whelping box. He was small, too, which made me feel less deficient in the size department. I was his favorite puppy and continued to lick his face far beyond what was age-appropriate behavior, just so he knew I liked that he picked me out as the best of the litter. I ran after him when he went in the house and stood up with my front paws on the screen door, scratching to let him know I was waiting for him.

My greatest hope was to be let into the house. Surely the boy would let me in if I was persistent enough. But it never happened. I stood with my tiny, black, pushed-in nose against the door glass, staring at my own image. At first I thought another pup from the litter was looking out at me, with his large, dark, protruding eyes and neat white band down the middle of his face, separating the black, curved bandit-mask that covered his eyes. It didn't take long to figure out that this apparition was me, since it whuffed, making the same noise I did. We made the same high, squeaking, sharp sound that humans tend to discourage for some reason I still don't get. I guess they wish they could do something besides endlessly chattering, using sounds that only once in a while made any sense to me.

When I was with Timmy, my little boy, I tried teaching him to whuff, but he couldn't master it. Just didn't have the right stuff, poor kid. When I made a high, warning sound, he thought it was the same as my friendly, let's-play whuff. The truth was that Timmy had no ear for dog-music, and I soon gave up trying to teach him. Instead, I whuffed with Dorothy and the two of us tumbled all over the yard, playing and learning how to explain the truths of life to each other and our littermates.

One of the great truths was the extreme desirability of chickens, both as playthings and as food. Another great truth is that pursuit and, worse yet, capture of chickens will get you whacked by humans. Being nobody's fool, I had noticed early in my life on the farm that humans chased chickens, chopped off their heads, and pulled out their feathers, a duty I would have been happy to carry out for them, had I been allowed. I suppose they ate the chickens once they were done with feather-pulling, another duty it would have been my pleasure to perform, but I was never given the chance.

I was going about my usual business, one day, digging here and there in hopes of finding a bit of cat poop or other fine-smelling dainties buried by fastidious perps, when I saw a car full of humans pull up and empty out. Now, I need to tell you that brave and large-hearted as I am and always was, I am cautious about new situations. I'm a thinker, and thoughts of the future are not always pleasant. Anyway, it occurred to me that this noisy bunch of humans might be planning to steal a puppy. That thought was confirmed by their fondling every one of my littermates stupid enough to get near them. I stayed well out of their way, warning Dorothy to do the same.

Our particular human, the farmer, was grinning and acting nicer than usual, all the while shoving the biggest and ugliest of the pups forward, probably hoping the noisy humans would take him. That would be Julius, my huge brother, who had never been a favorite of mine. When we were struggling for a teat, as I have said before, Julius used to put one large rear foot into my face, sending me tumbling backward. I still brood about that indignity and wish all kinds of retributive justice on my hateful brother. When we started getting milk in a flat metal tray, Julius was ill-mannered enough to step in with all four big feet and befoul the food with dirt. He did the same thing when the farmer began to give us kibble, kicking it around until hardly any was left in the tray. No, Julius was not my favorite pup.

Even when Dorothy and I whuffed our disapproval of his manners, he pretended not to know what our sounds meant and went right on doing whatever gross thing we had disapproved of. He even bothered Mother for milk, after the rest of us had politely quit trying. Julius would hang on her teat while she tried to run away. He was an oaf, I tell you, and I was ashamed to be related to him. Worst of all was our human's delusion that Julius was the alpha of the litter, just because of his size and rudeness.

The farmer made a big fuss over Julius, telling the visiting humans, "Now here's the alpha of the litter. Smartest of the lot. And the healthiest."

Burning with fury, I whuffed a protest, trying to communicate the truth. "He's no alpha, you idiot. He's dumb as a chicken and mean, too."

I was thinking that maybe Julius was so healthy because no feckless, uncaring farmer had crushed his bottom while pulling him out of the birth canal. And this farmer of ours was as much without feck as any human I've known. It was he who had the notion that tails were not useful to Bostons and had a vet lop ours off. I was too young to realize that one of my main avenues of self-expression was being taken away. For the rest of my life I have tried to wag the stump, but most people can't tell what I mean by it. That pisses me off, as my favorite human says when something annoys him. After the tail-lopping, I never trusted the farmer again. For all I knew, the next thing he would snatch would be my ears or my tongue or an even more vital part of my anatomy.

These visiting humans, probably because they, too, were dumb, understood nothing of my warnings. They bore Julius off triumphantly, as if he was the prize sow at the fair. Nobody was sorry to see him go. Dorothy and I did a little celebratory dance, standing on our hind legs until mine got sore, and I had to quit. We made quite a handsome pair, since she was only a little bigger than I was and almost as graceful.

I was not so happy when the next family came for a pup, because they were looking for a female. That meant Dorothy, the only female in our litter. Hearing the bad news from the corner of the barnyard that Dorothy and I defended as our own, I looked at her in dismay. It was a shock to my feelings for her that she looked pleased in a sappy sort of way, as if being female was something she had achieved by virtue of some superior moral worth. Although I tried to push her against the barn wall and lie on her in the dominating way of male dogs, she easily dumped me on my back and went running off to be admired by the visiting humans.

"Oh, you darling girl," gushed the lady of the family. "You'll be a perfect mate for our Mugsy. What cute puppies you're going to have!"

Just the thought of Mugsy making puppies with my Dorothy made me snarl and lower my head like a mad bull.

With a name like Mugsy, what could the prospective mate be but a lowlife cur, obsessed with perpetuating his kind on a helpless female? It was still possible to save her from Mugsy. Not being the descendent of pit-fighting dogs for nothing, I charged across the yard and flung myself at the woman who was attempting to gather Dorothy in her arms. If I were an ungentlemanly, biting sort of dog, I would have bloodied her hand, but being a proper Boston, I only worried it with my mouth and growled like a pit bull.

"Get this animal off my wife," bawled the father of the family. The children screamed and ran for their car.

"Wedgie, Wedgie," cried my own little boy, who couldn't pronounce his R's. "Be good. Let the lady alone." He darted over and grabbed me before I could make my point, the point being that Dorothy was mine.

I squirmed in his arms while the lady, intent on gratifying Mugsy's desires, bore Dorothy off to the front seat and her husband counted bills into the farmer's eager hands. Dorothy looked out the window as the car pulled away, and it seemed to me her mouth opened in a farewell whuff. I never saw her again except in my dreams. In them, I bit Mugsy where the sun doesn't shine and drove him off to whimper under a porch, while Dorothy and I played together in a grassy field bright with sunshine. More than once I woke up whuffing in a choked sort of way, my feet kicking wildly and my heart sore from missing my best friend. Happily, it was not long before a new best friend appeared, and he was not a dog.

Another pup was taken, leaving only three of us. By then I was two months old and well aware that my time at the farm would soon be over. I ran at Timmy's heels, hoping his love for me would prevent anyone from carrying me off to some uncertain fate. For all I knew, some family would come for me and drive me away in a car that would speed on and on, never to find a home. Although I liked a fast drive with my head out the window as much as the next dog, an eternity of driving did not appeal to me. I was beginning to want a place of my own, with a human of my own. Timmy was all very well as a friend, but he belonged to the farmer, not to me.

About that time, a very tall man with white hair drove up to the farm and asked the farmer to see his pups. The man's name was Frank, and he had a strong, deep voice that seemed to scare the farmer a little. Another alpha male, I thought. He might just suit me. I didn't run right over to him, since he didn't seem the sort to enjoy a lickspittle kind of dog. Instead, I let the other pups fawn over him and watched from a little distance, taking my time and thinking, as always. I sat on my tiny, mutilated tail and watched as the other pups tumbled over each other in an effort to entertain the visitor. After a few minutes, he looked at with a blue-eyed, piercing gaze.

"Come over here, little guy," he said, holding out his hand.

Okay, I thought to myself, not able to hold back. I was under the spell of those deep-set blue eyes and heavy white brows that came together in a masterful frown. This is it. My person. I ran to him and put myself in his hands forever.I was, as I've mentioned, very small, so small this man's hands could contain me. When he curled his fingers to make me a little nest, I just fit.

Yes, I said to myself. *Yes.* He held me up to his face, and I licked his nose gently with my tongue tip, not wildly slurping the way the others did. This was definitely it. Where Frank was, for me, was already home. We were a pack of two. I was in love.

Timmy cried a little when Frank took me away, but it was a done deal. Frank and I never looked back. There might be bigger, stronger Bostons, but both of us knew there were no smarter, larger-hearted Bostons than me. From the day I was chosen, Frank spoke of me as a flawless dog, the best. He didn't know about my rear end problems, and if he had, he wouldn't have apologized for them. I sat on the front seat of his car all the way to my new home, holding my small, round head high, enjoying the possession of car, human, and potential home. My name was Reggie, I was a king among dogs, and I had a human of my own. Life was good.

I learn to look away when my master eats

Chapter Two
The Bachelor Life

"One of his ears sticks up and one hangs at half-mast," Frank said to the breeder over the telephone. "Is he a dud or what?"

Frank sounded worried, so I was worried too. Something else was wrong with me besides my rear end. I wanted to be perfect for Frank and clearly I wasn't. I concentrated on my droopy ear and tried to make it stand up straight, but the muscle just wasn't on the job yet.

"It's okay, Bud," Frank reassured me as he hung up the phone. "Not to worry. The man says it takes time to get both ears up. Something about muscle control. You'll get it one of these days."

No amount of thinking about that ear muscle seemed to help, but after a few weeks, Frank looked at me with satisfaction. He held me up in front of a mirror so I could see for myself. The second ear was up straight, the tip slightly curled. I wiggled the ears and laid them back. Then I twitched them forward. My head worked a lot better than my hindquarters, I realized. From that moment on, I knew which end could be relied on.

Frank's home was much different from the farm. It was a small apartment above a golf course. My favorite part of our home was the balcony, where I could look out and see the geese swarm over the grass of the golf course in the evening and watch Frank play golf with his friends during the day. I longed to run after the little white balls he sent flying into the air, but that was not allowed. They had to lie on the grass and not be touched. Other balls were okay to play with but not these. I thought of them as sacred objects which Frank honored above all things. Except me, of course.

The less said about balls, the better. I was now of an age to be neutered, and Frank tried to prepare me for the ordeal. He sat me on his lap, looked into my eyes with his intense gaze, and talked to me, man to man. I don't say man to dog, since Frank always talked to me as if I was his equal, unless I had to be corrected. Since I was the sort of dog who wanted to please my human more than to eat or hump, I obeyed Frank as if he were God. He was certainly big enough to be God, at least in my somewhat limited universe.

For example, Frank is a light sleeper and forbade me to snore. Now, for a Boston, snoring is something that happens as naturally and inevitably as the sun comes up in the morning. My squashed nose prevented me from breathing silently, and as soon as I drifted into sleep, snorts would explode like Old Faithful. It was a genetic thing, I tried to explain to Frank. You buy a Boston, and you're going to get snorts. It's a law of physics. Frank was having none of it. My explanations did not move him. He insisted that I not snore. As always, I aimed to please. When Frank woke me up with the command to stop snoring, I learned to obey without interrupting my own sleep. Even my eyes stayed shut. But the snoring stopped, because God had ordered silence.

Bad things happen even to good dogs, I was soon to learn. Frank reluctantly bore me off to the vet, Dr. Mike, for the ultimate mutilation. Unlike the tail-lopping farmer, Frank took this melancholy event very seriously. He explained to me as we drove that I would benefit in the long run. No prostate problems, he said, assuming I knew what they were.

"You won't be frustrated when females in heat are around and you can't get at them," Frank explained. "That's very annoying, I can tell you from experience. You won't wind up lost somewhere because you were chasing an impossible dream."

I was more and more doubtful about the whole affair, since Frank seemed to have such strong feelings on the subject. His reassurances made me all the more sure that this was a bad idea, one which no self-respecting dog would agree to, if he had a choice. I laid my ears back, as I always did when I wanted him to know I didn't appreciate what he was saying.

"If I didn't live in an apartment," Frank said, trying to make me feel better, "there's nothing I'd like better than seeing you make puppies. But as it is, making puppies is out of the question."

His words reminded me of Dorothy, and I sighed, making a harsh coughing sound, my signal that humans should shut up. I tended to make this sound after receiving orders or corrections that I didn't see the reason for.

"Thwaash," I rasped. "Thwaash on that."

In this case, I was telling Frank that I didn't want to be reminded of puppy-making, since it brought back memories of Dorothy being taken away from me and sold into slavery to the gushing lady and her lustful Mugsy.

Of course, if Frank said neutering must be done, it would be done, and I would not make make a scene about it. Still, the deprivation he was talking about was all the more upsetting because I had never once had the experience he was referring to. Whenever he had a visiting female around, he would close the bedroom door, so I couldn't be part of whatever it was males did that I would never get to do.

We sat in silence, waiting for the vet. I remember Frank kept crossing and uncrossing his legs, as if they hurt. I pretended to take a nap, so as not to have to endure any more of his apologies and encouragement.

Later, after I woke up from a rather sickening kind of sleep, I found myself cuddled in Frank's arms, an unfamiliar pain somewhere under what was left of my tail. It was no worse than the discomfort I was used to in that general area, but I groaned a little and lay back against Frank's chest, playing the moment for all it was worth. In two days, I was myself again. If something was missing, I didn't know it. Actually, I felt more at ease and in control of my life. You don't miss what you never had.

In the evenings, Frank would take me out to play on the golf course, and I would chase ducks, who seemed to enjoy jerking me around. They would waddle away, just beyond where I could easily reach them, looking back at me coyly over their shoulders. When I rushed at them, they flew off, cackling with duck laughter, and settled down again, just where they had been before.

The resident geese were another story. They were none too happy with my attacks, and flew at me in a rage when I tried to play with them. Frank and the other golfers wished the geese would fly south and stop pooping all over the grass. The geese had no manners at all. I learned to be very careful about such things. When Frank opened the apartment door, I dashed down the steps and found a corner of the parking lot to do my business.

I must confess that initially I was not always perfect in regard to poop placement. When I first moved into the apartment, I was unsure about where to go, if you know what I mean. Finally, I found a closet in which Frank had left some smelly slippers that I thought would be suitable containers for my thrice daily gifts. He was not amused at finding something in his slipper that didn't belong there. I had mistaken the smell of feet for the smell of "potty," the word he used for my poop and pee. Mortified, I hid under his bed and wouldn't come out until he called me, said the magic word "potty," and opened the front door. Then I skittered down the steps and performed properly outdoors. I never made that mistake again, an accomplishment Frank often boasted of when other dog people complained that their animals had "accidents." In my view and Frank's, accident is not the right word. Criminal offense is more like it.

I was growing up into a dog that knew right from wrong, since my human was very clear on the subject. I learned to heel, to come when called, to shake hands, and most of all, to stand up for myself. Frank's morning ritual with me was to give me a boxing lesson. He cuffed, I feinted, and every day I became quicker in my reflexes. When he thought I was ready, he took me to a dog park divided into areas for small and large dogs. Now it was time to test me for my ancestral skills in the pit.

At first he put me with the small dogs, but they cowered in corners when I rushed them. So Frank opened the gate to the area for large dogs and let me go with them. I was pumped. What a hoot. I took off at my best speed, my tongue hanging out and my head lowered. The long-legged dogs ran so fast, it took all I had to stay close during the chase. I never caught even one of them, though they often caught and rolled each other. Finally, I had enough. Heaving and panting, I threw up my breakfast in a nasty little pile, signaling to Frank that this experiment was over.

"Forget about it," I said to him, in the only way I knew he would understand.

Despite my intelligence, my small size continued to be an issue for me. Still, my ancestry had formed me in such a way that I would never back down from a challenge; those ratters in coal mines and fighters in the pit had left me a legacy, and I wouldn't let them down.

Frank had a large family of humans who also had dogs, very big ones. As Frank had once believed, his family seemed to think that only when a dog approached the size of a pony was it worthy of respect. One daughter had a small boy about Timmy's size. He had wondered at my distinctive Boston features, asking, "What happened to his nose?" Once he understood that my nose was perfect for a Boston, he accepted me, despite my size. As I said, he had no experience with small dogs, and probably thought me a freak of nature. This boy, Kai, and I got on well from the start, except that he had a dog of his own, a giantess named Maggie. Frank and I visited Maggie's house when I was just a handful of puppy, but even then, the lines were drawn. I growled my tiny growl at her from across the room and lowered my head as menacingly as I knew how. She got the message and backed away a few steps.

Maggie was a Labrador, and very large. I could be an appetizer for this amazon, and I knew it. So did she, and it was her house. We stared into each others' eyes, as she made clear that I was to submit or else. As an alpha male, I was not going to take this challenge lying down. Well, actually, lying down was exactly the challenge. Maggie had a large, soft bed right next to the warmest place in the living room. I wanted that bed so bad I could have killed for it. But Frank would not look kindly on my murder of his daughter's beloved lab, even if I could manage such a heroic task. Craft was the only alternative to murder, and craft was my particular gift.

So I planned a subtle maneuver that only a Boston could bring off. I ran into the main bedroom and hurled myself onto the humans' bed, where I rolled ecstatically, moaning and kicking. Maggie came rushing in, determined to get me off the bed, which she had been taught was forbidden territory.

"Come on, dog girl," I whuffed at her. "Try to get me off this bed. Make my day." More moaning, more kicking. Maggie was out of her mind.

She stood up, her paws on the bed, her head darting at me, her jaws clacking in fury. She fell for the trap when I bit a pillow and shook it as if it was a dying squirrel. With a howl, she leaped onto the bed and pushed me off. Frank's daughter, hearing my calculated yelp of pain, came rushing in. She found Maggie on the forbidden bed, and banished the offending lab to the back yard, with some sharp words that made me chortle. I ran off to take over the warm, fluffy bed by the fireplace, and Maggie looked at me through the sliding glass door as if I was a nightmare come true. I rolled over on my back, made my trademark rasping noise of pure pleasure, and went to sleep.

After that, Frank decided to buy me a bed of my own. I had always slept in my crate, which was okay with me. A treat was always in there, and I could sleep without wondering if something bad like Julius was going to get me while Frank was asleep or away from home. Since Frank often took me out to run with him, I was grateful for a den to hide in and tired enough to enjoy it. The crate was my friend and protection.

One reason I loved my crate was that when I was in it, I couldn't see the squirrels that sometimes ran along the balcony railing, just to torment me. They would chitter, shake their tails, and drive me crazy. I couldn't help barking at them, though Frank did his best to discourage noise-making. The only way he could be sure I wouldn't bark and disturb the neighbors was to put me in my crate when he went out on mysterious errands, which could not include me. As long as I couldn't see the squirrels, I was quiet. In my sleep, I would seize them by the neck, one after the other, and shake them mercilessly until they were still.

Once, when I was in the parking lot doing my potty, a small squirrel dashed by and I couldn't help myself. I gave chase, pounced, and knew in waking awareness the joy of grabbing prey by the neck with my formidable, under-utilized jaws. Before I could finish the kill, Frank was all over me, squeezing my cheeks until I let the half-conscious baby squirrel go. He didn't scold me, knowing, I suppose, that it would be a useless exercise. I was a terrier, after all, and varmints were my instinctive enemies. One of the central truths of my universe had always been: their job was to tease and torment me by their very existence, and my job was to take them out.

But Frank apparently marched to a different drummer. He just shook his head, took the baby squirrel to a low tree branch, and sent my prey safely on its way home. I made my harsh cough, showing my displeasure, but accepted the inevitable. He was God, after all, and whatever his moral code, it must be obeyed, counter to mine as it might be.

Sometimes I could avoid Frank's code. One of those times happened in the yard of his younger daughter's home. She had a shepherd mix named Jonah, who was even bigger than Maggie. I found Jonah a challenge worthy of my best efforts. He wasn't the smartest dog in the pack, but he was easy-going and much loved by the daughter and all the family. My moment came when Frank was in the house getting some food. I always envied Frank's ability to get any kind of food he wanted, whenever he wanted it. Yes, he left a bowl of kibble out for me all the time, but it was hardly the equivalent of barbecued chicken. I grieved at this injustice, but knew better than to argue with it. That was one of Frank's favorite scoldings. "Reggie, you know better than

Well, yes, I did know better, but that didn't stop me from pushing the envelope whenever I thought I could get by with it.

From our earliest days together, Frank let me eat beside his TV chair, while he ate his own dinner. As he watched the screen, I watched him, wondering why he got to eat steak, while I had only kibble. I lay beside my bowl in such a position that I could stare hungrily at his plate.

After Frank had eaten his fill, he let me lick the plate. I lay quivering in anticipation until the plate was set before me. My staring while he ate began to annoy Frank. He looked down at me more and more often as I stared. Finally he ordered me to turn around while he was eating and face the wall. If I looked over at him, he knew at once, by some godlike sixth sense, and thundered at me to turn around. If I expected to lick the plate, I had to comply with his rule. After that test of wills, I behaved like a perfect gentleman, averting my eyes when humans ate. But in my dreams, I did unforgivable things, like knocking plates off tables, licking up food spills, and intimidating humans into giving me their dinner plates long before they were empty.

Family picnics, where many humans gathered, their plates heaped with goodies, I was not allowed to stare at, let alone pilfer. But if they were especially tempting, I stayed near-by. I might not be permitted to eat or stare, but I pushed the envelope in other ways. The trick was to press my luck without failing to please. Since I wanted to please Frank more than anything, I had to walk a continual tightrope between impulse and devotion.

At one family eating fest, Frank was inside, while the rest of the family sat around in the back yard. Jonah, the big shepherd, lay sprawled in the midst of them on the stones of the patio, snoring, his long tongue hanging out. Now, I thought, I will establish my dominance over this giant of my kind. Frank will be proud of me for my daring. He had served in the army and was well-acquainted with the glory of battle. I went for Jonah's back leg which was a lot bigger than me. And I began to hump until I realized that all the family was laughing and pointing. Then I stopped, not wanting to make a spectacle of myself or embarrass Frank, who was just emerging from the back door with a plate heaped full. I jumped off Jonah and ran under the porch. I was confused, smart as I was, and somewhat sad, feeling a lack I couldn't precisely define.

It occurred to me that this vaguely missed experience was what Dr. Mike, the vet, had deprived me of on that bleak day months ago. I was a confirmed bachelor, I told myself. To pretend I was anything else was ridiculous. From that time on until I came to live with a frisky little Bichon female, I kept my sex life a secret from Frank and from the humans who had laughed at me.

Tina and Tank share a toy

Chapter Three
We Enlarge Our Pack

Several years of life in the apartment went by uneventfully, punctuated by squirrel pursuit and runs on the golf course, but little else of note. I spent a good deal of time in my "house," as Frank called the crate. Frank thought I enjoyed it and kept me locked up for whole afternoons while he was out and about. I never complained, as I never complained of pain in my legs, but of course I preferred freedom. On several occasions, I took apart the crate from the outside, turning the screws along the sides until they dropped off. From the inside, though, I couldn't get at them. At least Frank supplied my "house" with a treat and a chew-toy, so I made my peace with the lock-up. It was the usual thing if a female came over, since Frank clearly had more on his mind at those times than amusing me.

Females came and went, but I didn't care. It seemed reasonable to me that Frank behaved with females like a sensible dog would, entertaining them for a time, then frisking off for an encounter with yet another female. It was impossible for me to grow attached to any of them, though most pronounced me "cute," and went back to making a fuss over Frank, while I stayed in my crate or behind a closed door. I made no connection with them and didn't care when they were replaced. Frank and I were a temporal constant, while the females came and went over the months.

After three years, Frank began to visit the home of a female who had the sense to say, "Bring your dog. I like him." She let her two dogs, about which more later, roam the house and yard instead of being confined in a crate. My crate, in fact, was retired to the garage at this time, and I seldom had to endure it again. Bee was the sort of female I could get along with. I liked the freedom, and the yard had grass I could nibble and roll in. I began to look forward to Frank's excursions to the Oregon coast and this female, Bee. Her dogs were mysteries to me, in that they did nothing but eat, sleep, and lie in laps. Frank called them "sissy dogs." Bee called me "the Boston Terror."

First of all, her dogs were Bichon Frises, lap dogs, curly and white. Tank and Tina, only a year older than me, were not exactly unpleasant, but they were not anything like a Boston, a fact Frank often remarked on, and not in a good way. Tank was fat and docile, so dumb that I once found him sitting in front of a porch door opposite the door with a dog flap. Admittedly, the two porch doors looked alike. But poor Tank sat facing the door without the doggy flap (which I must say had taken me only 10 seconds to master), and stared in confusion. I understood what he was thinking. *I could have sworn there was a doggy door here yesterday. Where did it go?* I ran back and forth through the door at the other end of the porch, trying to show him what to do, but couldn't make a dent in his dilemma. If the female human named Bee had not come along and positioned Tank in front of the flap, I think he would have stayed in one place, staring at the unflapped door until he exploded from accumulated pee.

And then there was Tina. She was half the size of Tank, just nine and a half pounds, lively, nervous, and unbelievably sexy. Frank called her "Freaky," because she barked at every shadow and startled at every sound. Tina had been rescued, she explained to me, from a horrible place where she had been kept in a cage and never allowed out. A puppy farm, she called it, not at all like the happy farm where I had grown up. She had neither toys nor friends and ate her own poop because hardly any food was dropped into her cage. I found this gross habit a little hard to accept, but tried to be a tolerant gentleman when I thought about it. Tina was, after all, adorable, even though she had eaten poop and wasn't a Boston.

While fond of other dogs, Tina hated most people, especially men in baseball caps. I couldn't quite get the picture, but the best I could grasp from Tina's hectic little mind-images was a scene of nasty boys poking at her with sticks and an absence of food. She told me that the only thing she cared about was freedom. Her human, Bee, had rescued her. Now Tina could go outside whenever she wished. For Tina, this favor was enough that she could tolerate being cuddled and caressed for short periods of time, but for the most part, this young beauty was seriously crazed and could barely tolerate being played with, let alone humped in the friendly, undemanding way I often proposed. I ran after her, pushing my nose under her rump, forcing her to run around the room on her front legs. It was all in fun, but she still thought I was a pain. When I bothered her too much, she leaped onto Bee's lap with a catlike cry. Actually, Tina was more cat than dog. In her early weeks, she had been raised by cats and loved them more than she could love a human or another dog, even her pack leader, which I was determined to be.

In time, Frank spent more and more time at Bee's house. That was fine with me since I was spending less and less time in the crate. I kind of got Tina's feeling that freedom was better than being caged. Together, the three of us played in the yard while Frank and Bee went off to do whatever it was they did without us. I wished Tank and Tina would play more aggressively, and they wished I was more laid back, but we learned to live with each other.

An example. A new couch was brought to Bee's house that offered a perfect place for both comfort and observing the street. Immediately Tank and Tina jumped onto the end of the couch with the best view of the street and tried to take possession. I was furious. No way, I snarled at them and jumped between the two. I sat up tall and stared them down as if they were no more than bugs. At that moment, though in deference to Bee I would not have bloodied them, I had the urge to kill. Both Tank and Tina took one terrified look at me and jumped down to the floor, never to occupy My Place again. From that moment on, I was pack leader and owned the sofa. Bee saw how it was and set up a table with pillows on it, just behind the sofa, for her two Bichons to lie on. It was higher than my spot, but less comfortable. I had made my point, as usual.

This same sofa got me into trouble soon after we moved in. One day Frank and Bee were out on some adventure, and I was on my own. I spent some time chasing Tina, who finally had enough and curled up next to Tank in an armchair and went to sleep. Since she was unavailable for play, I tossed my favorite ball around, chasing it wherever it rolled, capturing it, and then throwing it into the air. When it disappeared under the couch, I lay down on my stomach and stuck my head under the micro-suede skirt, looking for my lost toy. There it was under the sofa, just beyond reach of my paw. I struggled to nudge it, first with one paw and then the other. The sofa skirt kept getting in my way and finally I snapped at it.

Up till now, I haven't dwelled on my formidable jaws, normal equipment for a Boston, but only to be used in extreme circumstances. Bee called them the jaws of death, since once I had bloodied her hand by accident, trying to seize a toy. My potential for destruction was unimagined by my humans. Even I didn't know how much damage I could do, since I had almost always used my jaws in a gentlemanly fashion. This time, I forgot all my training and Frank's urgings to self-restraint. I went to work on the annoying sofa skirt, ripping it from the base.

Tank and Tina sat up on their chair, mouths agape, as they watched me growl and pull on the fabric. I let them know I wouldn't mind a little help, but sissy dogs that they were, they declined to enter the battle. Soon I discovered that if I chewed on the sofa base itself, tantalizing bits of fluff emerged which drifted around me as I plunged and pulled. By now, the sofa had taken on a kind of life and was, for me, a large and dangerous antagonist, intent on my ruin. Naturally, I had to destroy it first.

I suppose I knew better, as Frank later told me, but sometimes knowing a thing and acting in accordance with that knowledge are two different matters. My ability to think, which I like to believe is my distinguishing quality, deserted me, and I turned into a killing machine. If Bee hadn't come in the door at that moment, I believe I would have turned the entire sofa to rags and stuffing. But suddenly there she was, screaming at me as if I had killed and eaten her precious Bichons. It was only a sofa, I tried to tell her as she sat sobbing on her ruined furniture.

Frank found us amidst the scattered fluff and fabric, taking the whole scene in with one glance. He roared with rage and smacked my rear end, always my weak spot. It hurt more than he knew, but I didn't whimper. I had it coming to me and knew it. This time, Frank might not take my side, I had the sense to realize. So I leaped onto the couch and hid behind Bee. While she didn't exactly protect me, she explained to Frank that I must have been trying to get the ball which could be seen under the couch, just out of my reach.

Frank, being a ballplayer and sports-lover himself, calmed down, understanding that I had run amok in the interests of the game. "Sometimes," he said reflectively, "getting the ball is everything."Seeing that all was forgiven, Tina and Tank jumped off their chair and ran over to me, wagging their plumed, splendid tails in belated support. I wished they had not seen me get whacked, but my punishment was not a humiliation. Frank was, after all, our pack leader. Despite having jaws of death, I had to accept my status as merely his assistant. Being deputy pack leader meant that I was the one responsible for checking the perimeter of our yard, a task I performed twice a day. Occasionally I smelled raccoons and squirrels, but never caught one. My duties were complex and varied. I had to check the bottoms of Tank and Tina to be sure they had gone potty and weren't sick. I led the lot of us when Bee took us for a walk. If other dogs approached, it was I who barked and leaped at them, since in my opinion, this pack could not defend itself even if it had possessed weapons of mass destruction.

A particularly invasive squirrel really annoyed me. Frank liked the way it dove under the deck, carrying bits of food. He called it Fred and gave it a heap of peanuts, just to enjoy watching the squirrel stuff them into his face and stash them under the deck. When I came tearing out the porch door-flap to nail Fred, the squirrel would run up a tall tree in the corner of our yard and mock my efforts to catch it. I did my best to climb the tree, standing on my back legs and trying to jump. Though I hung onto the tree, my heavy chest pulled me down. Fred could do something that I, with all my brains, couldn't do. It drove me crazy. When darkness fell, I would slip outside and try to sneak up on Fred, watching the long, fluffy tail ripple and flip as the squirrel prepared its winter nest under the deck. From time to time, its head would turn and one bright little eye would glance in my direction, just to be sure I hadn't come too close.

One night I chased Fred up a tree and decided to park myself at the bottom. When the squirrel came down for breakfast, I reasoned, I would be there to catch him. Not understanding my commitment to this task, Frank finally came out in the middle of the night and bore me back inside. I protested with kicks and groans. The squirrel had won, at least for that season. Let him enjoy his nut-stash, I finally decided, once winter had come and the squirrel disappeared under the deck. When spring wakes Fred up, I'll be waiting for the little bugger, who will be too fat and sleepy to run, like Tank the Bichon, only small and edible.

Bee let her Bichons get away with murder. They didn't have to come when she called, unless they felt like it. They sometimes, if the weather was unpleasant, made potty in the house, to Frank's horror and mine. They lay in her lap and were endlessly combed, brushed, and cuddled, while Frank and I scorned them for being girly.

"Well, yeah," Bee said in their defense, "so we're girly. Anything wrong with that?"

Frank and I rolled our eyes, agreeing that being girly and a lap dog was an offense to canine dignity and common sense. I'm quite sure that Tank got more tummy tickles in a week than I got in my whole life.

We knew better how to spend our time. In the evening, we would go out and run together, leaving Bee and the girly dogs to their grooming and cuddling, glad to be who we were. If it was raining, and on the Oregon coast it often is, Tank refused to go out, even to potty, lest his curly white fur get wet and matted. Even Tina, who valued going outside even more than food or human company, didn't care for rain. With Bee's coaxing, however, she would leave the house long enough to do her business. Frank found their reluctance to perform basic outdoor duties intolerable and scolded Bee about it until she yelled back at him. They had basic disagreements about dog care, and poop placement was not the only one.

For instance, Frank had in his divine code of ethics the law that dogs played only with balls. Bee, on the other hand, felt that dogs should be allowed to play with whatever amused them, even if the toys were intended more for cats than dogs. She wrapped a small plastic pop bottle in one of her socks and let me toss, chew, and crackle the toy until the sock was ripped to pieces. She also created a toy on a rope that drove me nuts, a stuffed animal dragged about the room or yard that made me fight for possession of it. When I caught it, I would chew it to death, shaking it and growling. Tina sometimes tried to catch it, but Tank never bothered. Instead, he leaped on Tina and wouldn't let her play. In his view, Tina was supposed to play only with him, and never with me. If she dared to run around the house with me, Tank growled and pulled her tail, making poor Tina even more freaky than before.

It kind of reminded me of the way Frank and Bee acted together, sometimes yelling, sometimes hugging. Humans and dogs, we had become a blended family. Finally, Frank and Bee officially got married, and all the family came to see the deed done. We were a pack of five now. Tank and Tina were apparently mine to guard and put up with forever.

I, Tank and Tina inspect our turf

Chapter 4
Dogs in the 'Hood

The house we lived in was one of many in a senior community occupied by dogs and their owners, most of whom had white hair. They never jogged the way Frank did. Instead, they strolled slowly about the streets, stopping to talk to each other about their dogs. Bee's way of walking was to saunter along, allowing Tank and Tina to sniff at anything they pleased. She exhorted them to go potty and expressed great appreciation when they did, which Frank and I found ridiculous. If they had to go, he said, they needed no encouragement. If they didn't have to go, they should be obliged to move along at a rapid pace, eyes straight ahead, following their master on the left, as Frank had taught me to do.

If Frank said "heel," I immediately went around him to his left side and sat down, awaiting further instructions. Tank and Tina were clueless as to what "heel" meant, and couldn't care less. Tank waddled along behind Bee, while Tina pranced and jittered as far ahead as the leash allowed, looking from side to side continually, as if she expected a Doberman to attack.

Actually, the only Doberman around was a beautifully formed sable female named Shadow, who trembled at every sound or movement, and would not have attacked so much as a worm. She paraded grandly around the community at the side of her mistress, acting as if she was the protector, but I knew better. Just to see what Shadow would do, I rushed at her one day, growling and lunging. How gratifying it was to see her try to hide behind her mistress in total disarray. My habit was to walk in front of Bee and the Bichons in order to protect them from other dogs, especially big ones like Shadow. I had a reputation to maintain, and thought of myself as king of the entire community of dogs. One dreadful day, however, I met my match.

I had watched from my comfortable perch next to the window as the neighborhood dogs passed by on their walks and had seen a huge Airedale named Shelby trotting beside her mistress. At first sight, I determined that this dog was bad news. She had a way of holding her head too high and doing potty with some frequency in our front yard. One day, I thought, I would give her a lesson she wouldn't forget. Our paths didn't cross for the many months of winter, but when spring came, we found ourselves in the dog park at the center of the community. My pack and I entered, they behind me, and I very much in charge. Shelby froze and stared at me. I stared back, challenging her dominance. The scene was a bit absurd, I must admit, since I was barely taller than her kneecap. Still, we knew ourselves evenly matched.

We sprang at each other, growling and sneering, showing all our teeth. Bee and Shelby's human tried to stop us, but we were at each other before they could grab our collars. I went for Shelby's belly, since that was all I could reach. She let me get into position, then plopped down on me so hard I couldn't breathe. It was unsportsmanlike, given her superior weight. I sank to the ground in ignominy.

"Eee, eee, eee," I squeaked, sure I was going to be suffocated by this enormous beast who had crushed me under her. Only my head and front paws stuck out. I was flattened, splayed, unable to scramble free. How the mighty had fallen. My ribs and rear hurt. I gasped for breath.

The worst part was that the humans, including Bee, were laughing at me, pointing fingers and acting as if my predicament was a comic performance. Tina stared in shock and backed off, knowing she could do me no good, and Tank lay down on his back, waving his paws idly in the air, indifferent to the peril of his pack leader. I was utterly humiliated, deserted by my pack and alone. My reputation as strong dog of the neighborhood was in tatters, and Shelby was responsible.

Eventually, I struggled out from under the Airedale's belly and stood furiously panting at Bee's side, barking so hard my throat hurt. Still laughing, Bee fastened my leash and took me home. If I had dared, I would have savaged her ankles. When we got home, things got even worse. She told Frank what had happened, and imitated me with irritating accuracy.

"'Eee, eee, eee,' he squeaked." Bee laughed until she almost cried. "You should have heard him. Poor Reggie's ego was totally wiped."

My opinion of Bee dropped significantly, despite all the treats and walks she had given me. See if I would protect her next time a large, hostile dog was in the vicinity. She would have to take care of herself, I thought, putting my nose deep into a pillow on the couch and closing my eyes tightly to shut out the very sight of her.

Over the next months, I trained Tank and Tina to bark at Shelby when she walked past our house. Out of loyalty to me, they stood up on their hind legs at the window, just their barking heads visible to passers-by. Shelby turned in our direction when she heard the thunderous performance. She hurried on, not pausing to defile the front yard as she usually did. My pack and I had our revenge. We might be small, but when we barked together, we made more noise than Shelby could.

In a way, I felt vindicated, but ever after, I distrusted Shelby. When we passed each other on walks, she pretended to be friends, but I knew better and growled low in my throat. Someday, when she was weak, sleeping, or old, I would take her out, I consoled myself. Never mind if I would never again be allowed into the dog park. Shredding Shelby as I had shredded Bee's sofa would be worth any price I might have to pay.

The same park was the scene of yet another battle, this time one more to my credit. I was playing ball with Bee, who had found a squeak toy Frank didn't want me to play with. It wasn't a ball, and so did not have his approval. Still, Bee and I liked it. The thing was red, with two short legs, thick skin, and a squeak that could be heard around the block. I adored it. Bee threw it down the length of the dog park, and I caught, gnawed, and shook it until it had holes punched in its sides.

On this particular day, a Sheltie named Lucky entered the park. He was a cocky fellow, under the misapprehension that he was an alpha dog. Tank and Tina thought he was, but they, poor things, were only omega dogs and knew nothing of canine hierarchy. Anyway, Lucky was bold enough to run alongside me and attempted to leap on my two-legged ball. This maneuver was beyond tolerance, a challenge reminiscent of the infamous Shelby's. I had no choice. Bad as I knew it was, I had to bite him. Bee shrieked, and Lucky's owner snatched him up. I was pronounced a "bad dog," a label I knew would be relayed to Frank. Still, I held my ground, my head high, and my red squeak toy between my jaws of death.

Lucky's leg bled a little, which upset Bee, who made craven apologies and offered to pay veterinary bills. I couldn't explain to her that without blood, no lesson could be taught. She was furious with me and dragged me home to Frank. I was pleased that Frank defended me, saying that the red toy was mine, after all, and that any dog with a sense of honor would fight for his property.

The next week, I was finally allowed back in the dog park, after being reminded of my disgrace to the point of tedium. Lucky was playing with another dog, but stopped dead on seeing me come through the gate. I decided that if I was to satisfy Bee, I would have to make my peace with Lucky. After all, I had already established that I, not he, was the alpha dog. I could now afford to be generous. I trotted over to the Sheltie, stared him in the eyes, and lay down on my back in front of him, the first and last time I have apologized to another dog since I was a puppy, chastised by my mother.

Bee and Lucky's mistress both cooed and cried out praise for my gallant behavior. I wanted to explain that I was a Boston Terrier, a gentleman to the bone, but had no words. My actions would have to speak for me. Lucky nosed my belly and accepted my gesture. I leaped up and ran with him after a tennis ball that belonged to neither of us. Afterwards, we were the best of friends, but there was no question as to who was top dog. I had regained my neighborhood reputation as the 'hood's toughest dude, especially since no other Bostons were around to argue the point.

Frank and Bee decided I should have the chance to play with others of my kind, since most dogs were not my equals. They took me to Portland, where fifty Boston terriers took over a dog park once a month. It surprised my humans that I didn't immediately dive into action, asserting my dominance over all the dogs in the yard, as is my usual M.O. Instead, I stayed by the fence for a while, checking out the locals. Most of the Bostons, if not all, were larger than me, which gave me something to think about. Maybe, I thought, they were one large pack, with a super-sized Boston in charge, who could take out even me. My memories of Julius came to mind, and I decided to play it safe. For all I knew, the humans who had bought Julius thought it would be fun to bring him to this park and watch him throw his weight around. What I didn't need was another Shelby episode. So I lurked on the sidelines until I was sure Julius was not among the park visitors.

Finally I ventured out into the hectic sea of barking, chasing, wrestling Bostons. My humans probably figured I was going to enter into the fray, but I was actually looking for Dorothy. With so many local Bostons running around, wouldn't the odds be good that Dorothy was one of them? At least so I thought. I ran up to every female who reminded me of my beloved littermate and sniffed her to see if she was Dorothy, but no such luck. After a while, I just sat by the gate and brooded. What was the use of a park full of Bostons if my best mate wasn't one of them?

Bee and Frank tried to lure me into relationships with likely playmates, but I would have none of it. I knew they were disappointed, and was sorry about that. Since Frank and Bee had never known Dorothy, they couldn't have understood my reluctance to play with anyone else. The Boston Terrier day at the park, Frank and Bee had to admit, was an empty exercise, not one they would repeat. After a boring hour, they took me home, back to the little dog park in the 'hood, where I felt comfortable among my inferiors. I had to reconcile myself to the sad fact that I would never see Dorothy again, but would have to make do with the Bichons and other dogs in the 'hood. At least, I comforted myself over the loss of Dorothy, I would never see Julius again either.

Chapter 5
Things That Aren't Right

Over our four years together, I had taken Frank as my guide to what was and was not acceptable. His opinions became my own. His schedule was the same as mine. We arose late in the morning, took time to play our boxing game, which I was allowed to win, and finally emerged from our den to greet the day. Frank read his paper while I checked out the yard and the rears of the Bichons, just to make sure they had performed as they were supposed to. If Rama had dropped something unpleasant on the porch, I notified Bee, and she cleaned it up before Frank could see it and scold her dog.

In the afternoons, if the weather allowed, Frank and I would go to the beach, where I would run until my back legs ached. Frank never guessed that I was hurting. He took great pride in my endurance and speed. I never let him down. Sometimes I would see a distant dog that had to be investigated. I had a specific routine designed for unfamiliar beach dogs. First, I would crouch and look them in the eye. These stare-downs told me whether the other dog was seriously into violence or not. Given my size, I couldn't take the chance that the other dog had not been taught the social graces. If the beach was clear of dogs, I would then run too far ahead of Frank, but he trusted me not to disappear entirely.

Once I almost did. Our beach had a little creek running along the cliff beside it, and I ran across the shallow water, exploring. Frank was talking to some other dog owners as he often did and didn't see me disappear into the foliage beside the stream. I knew where he was, even if he didn't know where I was. All was as it should be, from my point of view. When I emerged from the foliage, having chased a slothful possum into a hole, Frank was nowhere to be seen. I trotted along in the direction of the parking lot, knowing exactly where Frank would eventually have to go. In the distance, I could hear him calling me, his voice sounding distinctly annoyed.

Knowing that it was Frank who couldn't find me, not I who couldn't find him, I didn't panic. Instead, I stationed myself at the base of the path up to the parking lot, aware that he could see me from the beach. It was only a matter of time. Finally Frank came storming up the beach, calling my name over and over, as if I might not know what it was he wanted. Across the sand dunes, he saw me, sitting and watching the waves, quite relaxed and in control of my situation. He scolded me only a little, since it was not, after all my problem but his that we had lost each other.

Yet another time, I ran well ahead of Frank on the beach, dashing around logs, sniffing at pee-mails left by other dogs. Such duties took time and effort. I couldn't expect Frank to understand that just as he read his newspaper, I, too, had messages to check out. He was jogging along slowly, looking at the waves rolling in, while I ran so far that he could no longer see me, nor I him. A lady was walking along the beach with her large dog, who looked to me to be a likely playmate. I preferred large dogs, since they could take my rough pushing and pouncing and nipping. Small ones tended to fold up or cry, bringing human retribution down upon me. This lady petted me, as humans always did, and said the silly thing that humans always say, 'who's a good dog?' as if they didn't know. Suddenly the lady grabbed my collar and attached a leash, telling me we would go and find my human. I was stunned. No one but Frank or Bee ever put a leash on me, and certainly never during a beach walk.

When Frank came trotting along toward us, he waved to the lady, explaining that I was his dog. It was almost as embarrassing a moment as the one with Shelby. I couldn't look at Frank. He was busy talking to the lady, who at last detached me from her leash. I stood behind Frank, hanging my head, wishing the large dog hadn't seen. He politely turned his face away and pretended to be watching the waves. I sometimes wish humans could be as respectful as dogs.

The beach was often in use by people with kites, since our Oregon coast was as windy, Frank said, as the Antarctic. Kites freak me out. Here were all these naïve, helpless people hanging on strings from sky-borne objects, and not realizing the danger they were in. The flying objects I hated most were the kind that swooped like birds of prey, darting and shrieking. They were clearly predators, and if unwarned, the hapless people could be either hit over the head or snatched up into the sky. Surely, I thought, they could see the problem. Since the humans made no attempts at self-protection, I leaped at the kites, barking and lunging, determined to save the humans in spite of themselves.

Sometimes the kites came down on the sand and lay there, helpless. Frank had to restrain me from murdering them where they rested. I wanted to explain to him that if I didn't kill them when I had the chance, they would fly up and work their malevolent will on these pathetically vulnerable humans. Without me, I was sure the beachgoers of Newport would have been picked off one by one, taken out by the pointed, swerving, noisy kites over their heedless heads. What bothered me was this: it just wasn't right. People should not hang from objects in the sky and that was that.

From the beginning of my association with Frank, I had determined that certain things weren't right. Like my master, I had strong opinions. Girly dogs were to be scorned; certain toys were unworthy of manly males; barking excessively at passersby was rude unless they were Shelby; pain was to be ignored; errors in poop placement by my pack were not to be tolerated. Frank and I knew the rules, even if Bee and her Bichons did not. They tolerated interruptions in routine that Frank and I found unacceptable. Sometimes they even took walks without me, since Bee claimed I pulled too hard and hurt her hands. These complaints drove me wild. I begged her to take me out on walks, turning circles at the door, grabbing Tina's leash to keep her from leaving. I tugged Tina all the way under the dining room table, trying to make it clear that unless I went out, she couldn't go either. Still, Bee and her Bichons broke my rules and left me whuffing and saying 'thwaash,' in fury when I was left behind.

At our first Christmas together, I taught Bee and her dogs a lesson. Since Bee thought her dogs were the ultimate in gentility, she tended to think of me as rather demanding and opinionated, like Frank, which of course I was. Being like Frank had been my goal from the time he took me home with him. It was important, I felt, to show Bee that I was a superior dog, just as Frank was a superior man.

On Christmas morning, the whole family descended on the gifts under the tree. Tank and Tina stopped short of the pile, uncertain what to do. We could all smell something good, but only I decided to plow into the presents for the one that was mine. I grabbed my gift and immediately tore the wrapping off. It was a chew toy that squeaked, just the kind I liked. Bee had obviously chosen it, since she didn't know squeak toys had to be really tough to withstand my jaws. I had the squeak out in a minute flat. Tina had watched me, and went into the pile to get another toy. She knew how to tear off the paper because she had learned from me, but getting the squeak out of the toy took her a bit of time. Poor Tank wanted a present too, but didn't realize how to get one. He stood hesitating by the gift pile until Bee handed him his wrapped toy. Not sure how to unwrap his present, Tank wandered around with it in his mouth for longer than I like to think about. I do believe that if I hadn't helped him tear off the paper, he would still be standing bemused in the middle of the living room with a wrapped toy in his mouth. Tank was a gentle soul and never cursed, as I would have, if I had a dilemma like his.

I had learned to curse from Frank, who didn't say 'thwaash,' but indulged in bad language of his own when he was frustrated. I rasped 'thwaash' many times when I wasn't taken out on Bee's walks. It was totally not right that I should not get my walk when the Bichons got theirs. Who would protect them from the Shelbys of the neighborhood, if not me? From my lordly perch on the sofa arm, I would watch the three of them move off slowly down the street, gnashing my teeth until my pack was out of sight. At least I had certain perks of my own, I consoled myself, and settled down to watch for their return. The sofa was not my only throne, off limits to other dogs.

I also had a soft, fluffy round bed that had belonged to a former dog of Bee's. When I came to live with her, the bed was up for grabs. Sometimes Tank or Tina lay on it, but they seemed not to know its worth. One night I dragged it into the bedroom, next to where Frank slept, and sank into it, sighing with pleasure. It made my sore legs feel better and supported the rest of my aching rear end. I felt like one of those kites sailing in the sky. Neither Tank nor Tina dared to contest my possession of the soft, round, blue bed. They might get more walks, but I had better places to sleep.

One day Frank decided to take my bed outside to get some sun, lest it become unhygienic. Many hours went by, and the sun started to go down. I went outside to do my final potty and was shocked to see that the bed was still on the deck, despite the evening chill and damp. I ran inside and said 'thwaash' several times to Frank, but he was watching football on TV and paid me no mind. I said 'thwaash, thwaash' loudly to Bee, but she was at the computer and ignored me. Tank and Tina had gone to bed for the night and, as usual, were no help at all.

Finally, Frank came into the bedroom. By then, I was beyond angry. I paced back and forth between bedroom and back door, 'thwaashing' furiously. I looked at the place my bed should have been and then looked up at Frank, rolling my eyes and making evil noises in my throat. I gave him what he and Bee called "the look," something I knew upset them.

"Oh yeah," Frank said at last, noticing that my bed was gone. "I see what you mean. You want your bed."

"Duh," I snarled. "Thwaash. I guess so."

That night I lay in my fresh-smelling round, soft bed thinking things over. I realized that humans could not be relied on all the time. They were sometimes late in putting out the food bowls, for instance, and occasionally forgot to walk us. My idea of routine was not theirs. Frank had a saying about putting up with what you couldn't change, and I tried to take this wisdom to heart. Breaks in routine were simply lessons humans and dogs had to learn, even though they weren't right.

I wait for Frank to put my bed in the right place.

Chapter Six
I Go to School

Frank had often bragged to Bee that I was the smartest dog he'd ever had, and he had had many. Most were large hunting dogs, but during his later years, when he lived in an apartment, a small dog was the only way to go. He had always made fun of men with small dogs, therefore this situation was somewhat embarrassing for him. So he chose a small dog that acted like a big one and had a face that announced its owner's toughness. He chose me. Sometimes he said I reminded him of a Boston he had enjoyed as a child, by the name of Pudgie, who had been remarkably clever. I did my best to live up to Frank's expectations. My smarts exceeded them, I am happy to say.

Language skills, for instance, were my particular gift. When Frank lay down on the bedroom rug to do his stretching exercises, he would tell me to go fetch a bone for myself. For some reason he was surprised when I did exactly that. I would turn over my little basket of toys and pick through them until I found just the right bone. Then I would bear it off to the bedroom to gnaw on, exercising my jaws while Frank stretched.

My old trick of shaking hands was outmoded. Frank decided to bring me into the twenty-first century and sat me down to learn the hip way to greet somebody. It took me about three seconds to get it. Frank waved his hand upward, saying, "High-five, Reggie," and I lifted my paw a tad higher than for the handshake, slapping it against Frank's hand. I was now cool, Frank said, and from then on, we greeted each other in no other way.

My athletic ability matched his, despite my injured rear quarters. When I tired of chewing, I lay beside him on the rug, usually on my back. I then wiggled around the edge of the rug, my feet kicking in the air. My next exercise was done on my belly, dragging my underside on the shag surface, stretching out to make myself as long as possible. I had given these exercises considerable thought and had come to believe that they would make me larger. Certainly Frank was larger than other humans, a fact I attributed to his hours of stretching.

Sometimes Frank underestimated my intelligence. It was his habit to send me out the doggy door late at night for a last potty time. Since the door to the porch was often left open in the evening, I was perfectly capable of going potty without being told. He realized this fact one night when he sent me out on a fool's errand.

"Time for bed, Redge," he said, pointing at the door. "Time for a last potty."

Now I had done a respectable potty in the yard on my own just a little while before, and Frank knew it. Nevertheless, I sighed and went out on the porch in the dark once again. I looked back at him, said "thwaash" as nastily as I could, rolled my eyes, and went out the door as instructed. Just to let him know he was out of line, I turned around and came right back through the doggy door, said "thwaash" again, and glared at him. He got it. No need to tell me when to potty. I was not, after all, a Bichon, but a grown-up Boston.

I had to communicate other things to Frank and Bee, letting them know I was an adult and capable of running my own affairs. One thing that truly annoyed me was the way Frank and Bee would look at me out the window in the morning when I was patrolling the perimeter, going potty, and checking to see that the local squirrel had not dared to enter our back yard. If I was doing my business, I always turned my head to see if I was being spied upon. When I saw them at the window pointing at me, I rolled my eyes, muttering "thwaash," and wishing I could tell them to get a life.

Frank decided that I was now so demonstrably smarter than other dogs I should attend agility school and enlarge my audience. He talked to Bee about entering me in contests and winning awards. I liked his boundless confidence in my abilities, but was a bit worried when he talked about jumping over hurdles and climbing up teeter-totters. While I could see the images in his mind as he spoke, the words were unfamiliar to me. Jumping and climbing sounded ominous, given the state of my back legs. Of course, Frank didn't know how bad they were, and I didn't want him to know.

Once, when he smacked me on the rear for some infraction of the rules, he really hurt me. I bit him, just hard enough to make sure he didn't do it again. The bite was apparently a miscommunication, since he whacked me once more, even harder. Biting humans was a crime, and I knew it. But he had caught me by surprise. The pain was too much, and I had reacted without thinking. Later, when he took me to a vet to have my hindquarters examined, Frank realized why I had broken this primal rule against biting the pack leader. I was glad to see he was sorry for what he had done. After that, Frank never hit me again.

The agility training school was a short drive inland, up a hill and beside a forest. It was dog heaven. Tina would have disappeared into the forest and never returned, but she was too nervous to go to school. All those strangers would have sent her into a frenzy of barking and skittering. Tank was too lazy to go to school. He would rather sleep in his chosen den under a corner table. I was pleased to be our family's only representative and I was determined to shine, however much the jumping and climbing might hurt my back legs. Nobody would hear about it from me.

Strangers were as much fun to me as they were terrifying to Tina. I was sure every one of them found me adorable, just as Frank always had. So I nosed and pawed each woman—for the agility school people were almost all women—until she told Frank how cute and friendly I was. The other dogs were mostly boring and shy, hanging behind their humans. I shone by comparison and was at once recognized as the "personality dog." My only real competition was a naughty standard poodle named Baxter, who was probably too young for this kind of training. He behaved with magnificent indifference to the wishes of the humans in charge of the class.

Frank and I would drive up to the parking lot, late as always. Bee often said Frank would be late to his own burial. When our car door opened, there Baxter would be, jumping all over Frank and trying to climb into the car with him. His abandoned owner would run after him, calling out apologies and orders. Baxter thought he was Frank's dog and acted on this assumption. He wouldn't leave for his agility training until we came with him.

Other dramatic moments made Baxter the bad boy of the class. We had to run through a tunnel that looked like a giant worm. It was an exercise I particularly loved. Frank tended to get the direction confused and to guide me into the wrong end. I had to be very patient with him when he messed up and to wait at the proper end until he figured out what we were supposed to do. Baxter cared nothing for the rules. Instead of running through the tunnel like the rest of us, he jumped on top of it and stood proudly wagging his tail, unwilling to conform.

One day Baxter committed the ultimate crime. I had just completed a perfect run-through of all the jumps, tunnels, and teeter-totter perches, when Baxter stole my thunder. He took off into the forest after a cat and disappeared for most of the class. The agility trainer and Baxter's human tore after him, fighting their way through underbrush and tree limbs while the class disintegrated into chaos. Most of the dogs ran around in circles, barking and chasing each other. I used the time constructively, practicing my routine, especially the tunnel, hoping Frank would at last understand at which end I needed to begin.

Baxter was finally dragged out of the underbrush, covered with little sticks and leaves, grinning hugely. His idea of a successful class was seeing how many mistakes he could make, while mine was the opposite. Still, we were friends, and I admired him for his originality. If there had been a class in breaking the rules, Baxter would have been the star, paws down. Sometimes, I thought when I reflected on Baxter's antics, it was okay if things were not right. The element of surprise added to the fun of the class, so Baxter got no bad marks in my book.

One day when I had been particularly brilliant in performing the agility routine, I felt an ominous rip and pain in my left rear knee. I had taken a hurdle too high, in the hopes of getting the humans in charge to raise the bar a bit. The height was suitable for Chihuahuas, maybe, but not for long-legged Bostons like me. On my way to the next test, a teeter-totter, I slowed a bit, trying to regroup. The pain in my leg was so bad I was reluctant to put my paw to the ground. Still, the show must go on, I figured, and headed up one side of the teeter-totter on all four legs, determined that no one would see my problem.

Frank was cheering me on, waving his hat and gesturing at the next hurdle, which happened to be the worm-tunnel. While I was inside, no one could see me, so I pulled up the sore leg and limped slowly through the tunnel. Frank met me at the other side, his expression one of confusion and a little annoyance. Why hadn't I come out fast, as usual? Hey, man, I wanted to say, my kneecap has swung around to west-northwest and the ligament holding it together is stretched fit to bust. You might give me a break.

I managed to keep the leg straight for the rest of the course, but was glad that the hour was almost over. Baxter came over and nosed me a little, then licked my sore knee. At least somebody had noticed, I thought. Humans had no clue. Frank just talked to the pretty lady who owned Baxter and dropped my leash, not seeming to care that I was about to crash and burn. He was bragging about how smart I was, and Baxter's owner agreed that I was the brightest dog in the agility ring. For once, I didn't care. I limped over to the car, hoping Frank wouldn't see my leg being carried at a crazy angle, and lay on the gravel under the door, wondering how I was going to manage the big jump into the front seat. If I failed, Frank would know I was broken beyond repair.

It's important to note that I had heard Frank say from time to time that a dog who couldn't walk would have to be put down. He had put down other dogs and was unsentimental about the basics. A dog had to be healthy, otherwise it was all over. I could gather from Frank's tone that any serious defect meant I was done for. He and Bee took me to a couple of vets, who did x-rays of my rear and my legs, then shrugged and wished my keepers luck. I was hopelessly defective in the back end, and no doctor could fix me. You can see why I did my best to hide my pain and pretend my ruined legs were no problem at all.

"I wouldn't even attempt the operation," one vet said. "His rear quarters are a total wreck. Maybe it's genetic, maybe an accident. But if I were you, I'd just enjoy having him around until his legs go, then put him down."

"He's only six," Frank said. "That's too young to die. Can't he just keep most of his weight on his front legs? I've seen him actually walking on them."

"Notice how his back is curved down in the rear," the vet replied. "It's called roaching, and it often happens to dogs with bad knees. The weight is carried in front as much as it can be and the chest over-develops. It isn't a good sign."

The thought of looking anything like a roach, scurrying around with a humped back, made me feel sick. So I was deformed, along with being in pain. Yet I could outrun any dog my size and many that were bigger. That had to count for something. I hoped it counted with Frank.

I heard another vet say, "The operation would be so hard that only the best orthopedic surgeon would try it. I wouldn't even know where to start. His back end is a nightmare. I don't think he could stand the pain of that operation. You might try getting one of those little carts that crippled dogs pull around behind them."

"Absolutely not," roared Frank, who always looked on the bright side. "He'll be fine. I know he'll be fine. Always has been." He chose to ignore the fact that I was more and more often carrying my left rear leg about three inches above the ground.

"Maybe we should go to the orthopedic surgeon up in Portland," Bee said. "Just to see if an operation could work."

"Anything's better than one of those effing carts," Frank muttered. "Yeah. Let's try a top-of-the-line surgeon. This little guy is too good to lose. We'll fight."

I felt better hearing him say that. Maybe it was time, I thought, to let him know how bad the pain was getting. Over the next few weeks, I kept holding up my sorest leg, the left rear one, as I walked. Now was not the time to worry about shame. Frank had to know I couldn't go on much longer. He stopped taking me to agility class and on walks during the day, when people could see me. I know it angered him that people felt sorry for me because of the way I held up my leg under my belly. He hated pity, and for Frank, pitying me was the same as pitying him. We were like one person. I did my best to keep the leg down when others could see me, but it hurt like hell. I was just about at the end of my rope.

I rest on my couch-throne, recovering from surgery.

Chapter Seven
I Go Under the Knife

"We're going to see Dr. Petersen up in Portland," Frank finally said to Bee. "I can't let Reggie go on hurting like this. He deserves whatever can keep him going. I don't care what it costs."

Apparently it cost a great deal. Bee said the cost didn't matter. It was just two trips to Hawaii that they wouldn't be taking. I agreed with her values. When a trip is over, it's over. But after this operation on me, they would still have a great dog. It was no contest.

The day before I left home for the surgery, Bee was especially nice to me, playing all my favorite games, letting me chase the mouse toy as much as I liked, even though Frank hated it. She looked sad and worried when she took me on her lap, and I began to get alarmed myself. Maybe the whole thing was a bad idea. Other dogs had told me about the pain of having a knee fixed, and I had a lot more going on than just a trick knee. I had heard Dr. Petersen, the famous orthopedic surgeon, say to Frank that metal plates and screws would have to be added to keep my kneecap in place, and that the bones above and below the knee would have to be taken apart and put back together. That's gotta hurt, I said to myself, and began to shiver uncontrollably, while sitting on my sofa-throne.

"He understands what's going to happen," Bee said to Frank, stroking my neck gently. "He really does."

I looked from one of them to the other, wondering if I would even survive the operation. Dr. Petersen seemed hopeful, but it was part of his job to convince dog parents that he wouldn't kill their kid. He said that ten percent of such cases as mine resulted in failures. His responsibility was to see that I wasn't one of them. The doctor said he had seen worse cases than mine, which seemed to cheer Frank up. He liked to think I was a wonder dog. Maybe this operation would prove him right. I could only hope.

Frank loaded my crate into the back seat for the long trip up to Portland. The crate was for after the operation, he said to me. On our trip to the surgery, he let me sit beside him in the front seat and even put my head out the window, usually a no-no. I had learned to press the button that opened the window and was pleased that Frank let me do it on this trip.

"You're going to be down for a while," he explained to me. "I want you to feel free now, while you can. Go for it."

So I hung my head out, enjoyed the feeling of the wind in my ears, and watched the cars fly by. I thought about the near-future, for I was, above everything, a thinker. This Dr. Petersen was going to do something horrific to my leg. It would hurt. I would have to be brave and not whimper. Frank would have to pay a lot of money and not whimper, either. I would do what was expected of me. More than anything, I wanted to please Frank, just as he wanted to get me back in shape. I was up for whatever it took.

The presence of the crate was a reminder that the operation would immobilize me for a time. I had come to prize my freedom, maybe because of Tina's influence, and wanted to tell Frank that I didn't need a crate. I enjoyed the passing scene, especially other dogs in cars. Most of them had to stay inside, not getting the full benefit of the breeze. Distractions were helpful, since the pain in my leg was getting so bad that whether I sat or lay down, I was in a world of hurt. Frank talked to me about what was going to happen, but what he said was so scary that I tuned him out.

"Dr. Petersen will make you sleep," he said, glancing at me as he drove. "You won't feel a thing when he opens your leg up. By the time you're awake, you'll have a whole new leg, better than it's ever been."

I had visions of the doctor removing my bad leg and attaching a new one. Frank's words confused me, and I shivered a bit. A new leg might be a good idea, but I was attached, you might say, to the old one, and didn't want to let it go. As I waited with Frank in the hospital, I licked my bad leg obsessively, trying to reassure it that I would defend it as best I could. Of course, I could do nothing, once humans took over. It was one of the things I hated about being a dog.

No turning back now. Dr. Petersen, all dressed up in a green hat and long green coat, came out to get me. You may have heard that dogs can't see color, but I'm telling you, some can, and I'm one of them. Green is a good color, I've always thought. It's the color of grass, which I like to eat and roll in. Now it would have other, less pleasant associations for me.

"You'll remember not to let him walk, jump, or play for two months," he said to Frank. "Any jarring could undo the whole effect of the surgery."

I looked from one of them to the other in disbelief. Two months without any fun? Without any work? Who would guard Tank and Tina? Who would leap onto the sofa and bark out the window at trespassing dogs? The whole pack would fall apart without my constant surveillance. Except for Frank, none of them could so much as take a walk around the block without risk of being mauled by any passing hound, if I wasn't on hand to protect them. Frank was often away on business or "working out," whatever that was, leaving Bee and her pathetic Bichons at the mercy of any passing man or beast.

Although our neighborhood seemed reasonably safe, I knew that large dogs might lurk behind bushes and could easily pull away from their frail old masters. I could picture Shelby falling savagely upon Tank and Tina while I lay helpless, immobilized in my crate. My pack would be easy pickings without me there to warn aggressors off. The thought of Bee sobbing over her mangled sissy dogs drove me into making a long, sad howl of distress. Frank and Dr. Petersen looked at me in surprise.

"It's okay, Reggie," Frank said in his deep, soothing voice. "You'll be just fine. Dr. Petersen's going to fix you so you can play again."

Frank didn't understand that I wasn't so much worried about myself as about my pack. I whuffed and moaned, trying to explain that while I was out of action, he had to make sure Tank and Tina remembered not to foul the porch in rainy weather, to check the perimeter of the yard for squirrel incursions, and to warn off enemies like Shelby, who would certainly use my absence to savage my helpless Bichons as she had me. If Shelby could squash a Boston, I could only imagine what she would do to Tank and Tina, given the opportunity. I rolled my eyes at Frank, fixing him with the dreaded "look," hoping he understood that the pack's safety was now up to him alone.

"Bostons are brilliant dogs," Dr. Petersen said, scooping me up under one arm. "I've known a lot of them. This one is special, I can tell. We'll take good care of him."

It crossed my mind that this moment with Frank might be my last. For all I knew, the whole scene was a performance to distract me from being "put down," in the usual way of defective or dying dogs. I moaned a little and kept my eyes on my master as I was borne off to be put to sleep or to death, whichever it was to be. Frank waved and smiled rather feebly, I thought. His eyes looked different, kind of wet and sad. I tossed my head and whuffed a farewell. If I was done for, at least my master would know I had been gallant to the end. He would remember me as a fighter, the kind of dog he respected.

For Frank, respect was everything. He couldn't stand wimps. If I could have saluted, I would have, but instead I waved my paw, in a gesture like the high-five he had taught me. Then Dr. Petersen bore me away into an all-white room, where other humans were waiting, also dressed in green. I suppose they thought dogs would enjoy seeing the color of grass before they went under the knife.

The lights were too bright for me, and I blinked. My eyes and nose were running, and a lady with a mask on wiped them gently. Then she put a mask on me as well, and I breathed in a sweet, unpleasant smell that reminded me of other painful moments. I had already lost my manhood and my tail, I thought dizzily. What will they take from me this time? Please, not my leg. Painful and shaky though it was, I was used to that leg and wanted to keep it. I had seen three-legged dogs hobbling around and didn't want to be one of them. My last mental image as I drifted off into a restless sleep was of myself without my left rear leg, trying to balance on the right, which was almost as damaged as the one the doctor might, for all I knew, be about to cut off. Or, he might be putting me down having conned Frank into believing that he meant no harm. I gave a final, weak whuff of protest as I fell into oblivion.

I woke up in a cage, feeling groggy and about to barf. Right away, I checked to see if I still had my left leg. Good. It was there, but covered with a white patch and hurting worse than it ever had. Thanks a lot, Frank, I said to myself. Yo, Dr. Petersen, I think Frank paid you to fix the leg, not make it worse. Oh thwaaash, I'm dying here. How about some meds, people? I moaned out loud. A pretty nurse named Jackie came over to my cage and cooed at me. I moaned again, hoping for something to eat, something to stop the pain. I felt like I had been starved for days, and my mouth was dry as a beach. Jackie opened my cage, gave me a spoonful of mushy stuff which immediately made me dizzy and weak. I fell over on my right side, sure that she had decided to kill me again, since it hadn't worked the first time.

All around me were other dogs in cages, some sleeping, some howling, some just making sad little sounds. At least we weren't dead. Or maybe we were, and didn't yet know it. My leg felt as if Shelby had gnawed it into hamburger, and the thought afflicted me that I might never get revenge for this final insult. As I fell into a deep, healing sleep, I thought of Frank, remembering when I had been a tiny pup in his large hands. I could almost hear his voice saying, 'It's okay, little Bud. I'm here.'

The next day, he really was there, talking to Dr. Petersen, who had put me on a table, like I was something for dinner. Frank patted my head as he spoke to the doctor and looked at my bandaged leg with a frown.

"No splint or anything?" Frank said. "What if he hurts himself?"

"That's your job," the doctor said. "I've done mine. Yours is just to keep him quiet. No jumping or playing or running."

Yeah, right, I thought. Like that's going to happen. I've got work to do at home. How I was going to do it, with my leg burning and aching like it was being torn off, I had no idea. But the worst was over. I was alive, my leg hadn't been taken away like my tail and my unmentionables, and Frank was holding me in his arms again. Jackie the nurse came out to say good-by. Just to show there were no hard feelings, I licked her nose when she bent over me.

All the way home, I slept in my crate, not caring about windows and wind. Soon I would be with my pack and all things would be as they were. I hadn't bargained for the pain and the inability to jump onto my couch-throne. When Frank brought me in the house, I couldn't stand up. It was a humiliating scene. Tank gazed at me vacantly, maybe wondering where I had been, but likely thinking nothing at all. Tina rushed over, wagging her tail, sniffing at my nose, then at my bad leg. I hated for her to see me like this, but at least she cared. Bee carried on like I was dying, and held me on her lap for hours. I was home, and felt glad, despite the increasing pain. What had that doctor done to me, I wondered? Why had Frank let him do it? This pain was worse than anything I'd ever had before. I wanted to tell Frank he had paid too much, given that the doctor had made me suffer more, not less. Seeing that I felt terrible, he held my mouth open, popped in a pill, and I went to sleep again, blessedly feeling nothing.

A few days went by, when I had to be carried out to do my business and couldn't walk at all. I was too miserable to care if Tank and Tina saw me being pathetic. They stared and were quiet, not coming near me. It was just as well. If any dog had so much as touched me, I would have bitten his nose off. Bee fed me a little bit, but mostly brought me my medicine in a glob of peanut butter, a treat I loved. It was all that made life bearable. Even when the pain got better, all I could think of was my peanut butter and meds fix.

Sometimes I lay on my soft, round bed, now in the living room by the TV chair, and whimpered, just so Bee would come in and give me my drug. I had her well-trained. She would come into the room and I would shiver and moan, then lick my bandage. Bee would run to the kitchen to fetch the wonderful meds. It worked like a clock. Shiver, moan, and get the meds.

Frank watched Bee stuff me with peanut butter and the woozy-making stuff inside. "He's playing you, don't you see? This dog is totally wasted."

I lay on my bed, tongue hanging out, grinning a little, helpless against the sweet effect of my peanut-butter drugs and went to sleep, happy and pain-free.

After the first week, I started coming back to life. Bee cut back on the meds at Frank's command. I was busted. The pain was still bad, but I could walk around the house. When Bee and Frank weren't looking, I jumped up on the sofa. I went out on my own through the doggy door to do potty. Bee wondered if I should be tied down. Frank said no.

"He's using his muscles again," Frank said. "Let him do what he wants. It's good for him to do whatever he can." To his way of thinking, it was always more therapeutic to exercise than not, whatever the pain.

Frank took me on short walks, though he wouldn't let me run with him on the beach, as we used to do. One day, when I was limping along, my bad leg held above the ground, I saw Shelby in the distance. Oh, you bitch, I thought. You think now is your moment. Despite the pain, which I must say was extreme, I put my leg down. It wouldn't do to have Shelby think I was weak and helpless. That would bring out the worst in her, all my instincts told me. She would be all over me, like last time. But Shelby passed by, wagging her tail. I was sure she knew something was wrong with her enemy, but was playing the hypocrite in order to please her kind mistress. Given another scene, she and I would be duking it out in the dog park, Shelby taking advantage of my weak leg. Luckily, Frank had listened to Dr. Petersen. I couldn't go to the dog park, couldn't run, and couldn't play. The ultimate battle with Shelby would have to wait.

Although I wasn't allowed to play, I could hop around the house and take short walks. That is, until Frank took me back to Dr. Petersen, two weeks later. The doctor read Frank the riot act. For the next month, nothing but short leash walks and being stuck in the crate.

"He loves his crate," Frank muttered. "No problem."

"I told you so," Bee said. "He should never have been running around."

Frank held me on his lap and denied any wrong-doing. "He's fine. No problem."

That was always Frank's view. Everything was fine. Bee assumed the worst. Maybe it was something she had learned from having Bichons. Tina, raised by cats and puppy farmers, was certainly a pessimist. Life in a crate had taught me she had a point. When I wasn't locked in the crate, the temptation to jump up on Frank's big TV chair was sometimes too much for me. He tended to spill bits of food there, and I considered it my job to mop up after him. At the end of my third week of recovery, Bee and Frank were out of the living room, so I felt free to jump into the chair and root around for tidbits. Frank came roaring in suddenly, and Bee followed close behind. I peeked over the arm of the chair, then shrunk down as small as I could make myself. My ears lay back, flattened against my head, as they always did when I was scolded.

"You were supposed to be watching him," Bee yelled. "You were supposed to attach his leash to the foot of the chair to keep him down. Now look what he's done."

"I thought he was in the kitchen with you," Frank yelled back.

Both of them sounded like they were going to dump on me after they finished dumping on each other. I hate being dumped on, since my main rule in life is to please my humans. At once I began to shake all over and kept my ears laid back as flat as I could. This was my signal to Frank that I was abjectly sorry for whatever it was he thought I had done wrong. Often I didn't know exactly what that might be, but the extent of the yelling and dumping told me that this time I was really in trouble. Finally Bee stopped blaming Frank and picked me up, examining my leg with cool, gentle fingers.

"I can't feel anything wrong," she said cautiously, then went on in her usual pessimistic way. "But how would I know if there's been internal damage?"

Frank muttered something about her borrowing trouble all the time, and she countered that he lived in La-la land. Pretty soon I found myself in my crate with some palliative beef jerky, while they argued about something else. I guess I'd gotten them all worked up, so they had to let off some steam, kind of like when I bit Lucky. Humans don't bite; they yell, or at least that was the conclusion I drew from watching mine get excited.

Shelby, Frank, and Me

Okay, we're friends now, but this dude is
my dad, not yours

Chapter Eight
My Comeback

About a month after the operation, I felt good enough to put a bit of weight on the leg. It was only a test, I wanted to explain to Frank, who kept exclaiming that I must be all well, if I could walk right. I wasn't well, but I could fake it when I wanted to. My first venture into normalcy occurred when Tina had just been groomed and looked exceptionally gorgeous. She was all fluffed up and her golden-brown eyes shone in her white face. What a dish. Whenever she was groomed, she turned me on, and now was no exception. Damn the leg, I thought. I'm going in. I took off after her and put my nose under her rump so that she had to run on her front legs. It was my favorite maneuver, one that established my dominance and made Tina know she was mine, whatever fuss Tank might make.

"He's back!" Frank crowed to Bee.

And I sort of was. From that moment on, my humans had to fight to keep me quiet. I ran to the water bowl, to chase Tina, to look through the window and bark warnings at passing dogs. I hovered around the book shelves where forbidden toys were kept, especially when Frank went out. Bee gave me the two-legged red ball for chewing. She put on my favorite TV shows, something called "Winged Migration," featuring birds that flapped and squawked as they soared over the hills. I couldn't take my eyes off them. I watched polar bears tear apart seals, imagining that I could swim and hunt like them, if only I lived on a little screen. It was a substitute life, but better than lying there licking my paws out of boredom. They had turned red from my tongue's attentions. Frank put something called "Bitter Yuck" on them, which made me say "thwaash" in fury at the acrid smell and taste. It was going to be a long month.

Often Frank would take me to the gym where he worked out, leaving me in the car to think my own thoughts while he had fun. Usually I slept, since no amusement was available, and Frank told Bee how I pulled a blanket over myself using my teeth, thinking this feat remarkable. Why he thought so, I couldn't quite work out. It was cold; I required a cover. Duh.

My humans had chosen winter as the best time for my recovery period, and they were right. The rain never seemed to stop. I lay on my sofa-throne and stared mournfully out the window, thinking that the weather matched my mood. Sometimes Shelby came by and stared at me when I barked at her, daring me, I guess, to come out and fight. Yes, she would have liked that, squashing me once again. This time it would be easy, since I couldn't put my full weight on my bionic left leg. One of these days, I thought, this leg is going to be so strong I can jump right over Shelby. I daydreamed about landing on her back and biting her ears while she bucked and thrashed, unable to throw me off. In my dreams I accomplished astounding feats of bravery, hanging onto Shelby's fur as I went for her neck. I dreamed that she tried to roll over onto me, but I leaped off just in time, then leaped on again when she was back on all fours.

During my recovery, Tank had reported dutifully to me, remarking on any passing dogs and any incursions by squirrels in the back yard. He found an empty peanut shell in the yard and brought it in, laying it at my feet. That item told me that winter was over and Fred had come out from the winter sleep, leaving signs of passage. It was time I rose up and made ready for battle. My leg no longer hurt, and I knew I was the equal of any attacker.

Finally the day came when Bee took me out to walk with the other two dogs. I trotted ahead of them, proud to be back in charge. We had barely entered the dog park when I saw Shelby coming in from the other end. I froze and would have dropped my tail down, if I'd had a tail.

She lowered her large, rectangular head until her beard touched her chest and came forward slowly, her eyes fixed on mine. She wanted a contest, I thought. She's begging for trouble. Bee called out cheerfully to Shelby's mistress, not grasping that friendship was not going to happen. It was war. I growled low in my throat, and both Tank and Tina growled too, hanging behind me for protection. My troops were nothing to brag about, but at least they had my back. That Shelby was bent on taking me out, I was sure. That I was ready, I had no doubt. Bring it on, bitch, I said to myself, bring it on.

To my surprise, however, when Shelby came closer, she neither snarled nor bared her teeth. She sniffed the air and her furry eyebrows drew together as if she was engaged in heavy thought. I stood my ground and didn't move as she approached, waiting for her signal to begin the fight. Bee might never walk me again if I was the first to start trouble.

Then Shelby inspected my leg, the one that had been shaved, but now looked almost normal, the long surgical scar having disappeared under re-grown fur. Since she made no threatening move, I held still, waiting for the attack I was sure would come. But Shelby acted in a way I could hardly believe. She licked my leg with something like tenderness. Then she cocked her huge head to one side and looked at me as if for the first time. Next she put out a paw and touched my head lightly.

"She's acting like Reggie is one of her pups," said Shelby's mistress. "She's trying to take care of him."

And so she was. I'd gotten it wrong all this time. Shelby meant me no harm. Whatever had happened between us was forgotten. If my miserable winter had been nothing else, it had at least helped Shelby and me to become friends. Well, maybe not best buds, but certainly not enemies.

My secret wish had always been to be considered a big dog, in spite of my small body. When Shelby adopted me as if I was one of her pups, I felt as if I had finally come into my own as a dog of formidable size. I had always longed to play with big dogs worthy of my attention. Frank had taught me boxing strategy and I was eager to test my skills on Shelby, who would not collapse like a wet noodle the way little dogs do.

I gave her a tentative poke in the snoot, then backed up, veering away from her as she leaped at me. We chased each other around the dog park until both of us gave up, panting and overheated. I lay down and put my legs in the air, signaling a time out. Shelby did the same, lying down on her back beside me, companionably kicking her long legs. Bee remarked to Shelby's human that the lion had finally lain down with the lamb. I hoped she meant I was the lion, but was content to let the issue drop. Thinking is not, after all, of utmost importance in the life of a dog, even a dog of superior intellect, such as I am.

Shelby nudged me with her furry muzzle. "You okay?" she whuffed in my ear.

"I'm good," I whuffed back. And I was.

I Call it a Day

Tails to Come

Since I am only seven at this point, many new
adventures lie ahead. Bee tells me she will
put them on our blog from time to time.
You tell me yours and I'll tell you mine. Whuff!

Reggie Wilson

wilson@spiritbooks.me

CPSIA information can be obtained at www.ICGtesting.com
Printed in the USA
LVOW08s2301211114

414958LV00003B/155/P

9 780983 495659